ELLIOTT CARTER

MNEMOSYNÉ
for Solo Violin

HENDON MUSIC

BOOSEY & HAWKES

AN IMAGEM COMPANY

DISTRIBUTED BY

HAL•LEONARD®
CORPORATION
7777 W. BLUEMOUND RD. P.O. BOX 13819 MILWAUKEE, WI 53213

www.boosey.com
www.halleonard.com

COMPOSER'S NOTE

Mnemosyné was composed for the extraordinary violinist Rolf Schulte for my 103rd birthday concert on December 8, 2011 in New York City. It is dedicated to my wife Helen.

– Elliott Carter

NOTE DU COMPOSITEUR

Mnemosyné a été écrit pour le violoniste extraordinaire Rolf Schulte à l'occasion du concert anniversaire de mes 103 ans le 8 décembre 2011 à New York. L'œuvre est dédiée à ma femme, Hélène.

– Elliott Carter

ANMERKUNG DES KOMPONISTEN

Mnemosyné wurde für den aussergewöhnlichen Violonisten Rolf Schulte anlässlich meines 103. Geburtstagkonzertes, das am 8. Dezember 2011 in New York City stattfand, geschrieben. Es ist meiner Frau Helen gewidmet.

– Elliott Carter

Duration: 2 minutes

for Rolf
MNEMOSYNÉ
for Violin
Remembering my wife, Helen

Elliott Carter
(2011)

NYC 11/17/11

ELLIOTT CARTER
(1908–2012)

Composer Elliott Carter is internationally recognized as one of the most distinguished American voices in classical music, and a leading figure of modernism in the 20th and 21st centuries. He was hailed as "America's great musical poet" by Andrew Porter and noted as "one of America's most distinguished creative artists in any field" by his friend Aaron Copland. Carter's prolific career spanned over 75 years, with more than 150 pieces, ranging from chamber music to orchestra to opera, often marked with a sense of wit and humor. He received numerous prestigious honors, including the prestigious Pulitzer Prize on two occasions: for his String Quartet No. 2, 1960 and String Quartet No. 3, 1973. Other awards include Germany's Ernst Von Siemens Music Prize, and the Prince Pierre Foundation Music Award. Carter was the first composer to receive the United States National Medal of Arts, and was one of a handful of composers elected to the American Classical Music Hall of Fame. He was recognized twice by the Government of France: named Commander of the "Ordre des Arts et des Lettres," and received the insignia of Commander of the Legion of Honor in September 2012.

Born in New York City on December 11, 1908, Elliott Carter was first encouraged toward a career in classical music by his friend and mentor Charles Ives. He studied under composers Walter Piston and Gustav Holst while attending Harvard University, and later traveled to Paris, studying with Nadia Boulanger. Following his studies in France, he returned to New York, and devoted his time to composing and teaching, holding posts over the years at the Peabody Conservatory, Yale University, Cornell University, and The Juilliard School, among others.

Carter's early works demonstrated a neoclassical style, highlighted by masterpieces such as Symphony No. 1 (1942) and *Holiday Overture* (1944), influenced by his contemporaries Copland, Hindemith and Stravinsky. After 1950, he shifted his compositional style away from neoclassicism and developed a unique and signature rhythmic and harmonic language, often using tempo modulation. Igor Stravinsky hailed his Double Concerto for harpsichord, piano and two chamber orchestras (1961) and Piano Concerto (1967) as "masterpieces."

Carter wrote many pieces based on literature or poetry over the span of his career, setting texts by acclaimed American authors and poets, such as John Ashberry, Elizabeth Bishop, E.E. Cummings, Robert Frost, Wallace Stevens and William Carlos Williams. A creative burst of imaginative works began in earnest during the 1980s, with works such as *Night Fantasies* (1980), *Triple Duo* (1983), *Penthode* (1985), and major orchestral essays such as Oboe Concerto (1986–87), *Three Occasions for Orchestra* (1989), Violin Concerto (1990), and *Symphonia: sum fluxae pretium spei* (1993–96). Carter's only opera, *What Next?* (1997–98) was introduced by Daniel Barenboim, a champion of the composer's music, in Berlin in 1999. Carter's remarkable late-career creative burst continued at an astonishing rate, with more than 60 works coming after the age of 90, with major additions to the modern repertoire, including his Cello Concerto (2000), *Of Rewaking* (2002), *Dialogues* (2003), *Three Illusions for Orchestra* (2004), *Mosaic* (2004) and *In the Distances of Sleep* (2006).

Carter celebrated his 100th birthday in 2008, a year marked with salutes and tributes at concert venues and music festivals around the globe. On the occasion of his birthday, New York's Carnegie Hall presented a new work, *Interventions* for piano and orchestra (2007), performed by the Boston Symphony with James Levine and Daniel Barenboim.

In his final years, Carter continued to complete works with astounding frequency. His Flute Concerto (2008) was premiered by Emmanuel Pahud and the International Chamber Music Ensemble; *What are Years* (2009), commissioned by the Aldeburgh and Tanglewood festivals; and *Concertino for Bass Clarinet and Chamber Orchestra* (2009), premiered by Virgil Blackwell and Toronto's New Music Concerts Ensemble. An all-Carter concert in honor of his 103rd birthday in December 2011 featured the world premieres of *String Trio* (2011) and *A Sunbeam's Architecture* (2010), as well as two surprise pieces composed in the month preceding the concert: *Rigmarole* and *Mnemosyné*. Among Carter's final works are *Dialogues II* (2012), a concerto for piano and orchestra dedicated to Daniel Barenboim and premiered just weeks before his passing at the age of 103, and *Instances* (2012) for the Seattle Symphony.